William Hunt

A LIFE OF DEVOTION

Family History StoryBooks

William Huntington Jr. was born in the small town of New Grantham, New Hampshire, in 1784. Growing up in a rural setting, he learned the value of hard work and resilience. At the age of 20, William decided it was time to start his own family and future.

In 1806, he married Zina Baker, a kind and hardworking woman. Together, they moved to Watertown, New York, seeking new opportunities. Their journey marked the beginning of many adventures and trials that would test their faith and strength.

Despite the challenges of frontier life, William and Zina's love and commitment to each other never wavered. They were ready to face whatever came their way, supporting each other through thick and thin.

The War of 1812 brought many hardships to William and his young family. He played the fife and fought in one battle, but the conflict took a heavy toll on their farm, leaving them in financial ruin. Despite these setbacks, William's determination never faltered.

After the war, William worked tirelessly to rebuild his farm. His efforts paid off, and soon he was a prosperous farmer once again. The Huntington family grew with the addition of four daughters and six sons, bringing both joy and sorrow into their lives.

Tragically, one daughter and one son passed away before reaching adulthood. The losses were deeply felt, but William and Zina found strength in their faith and each other, continuing to provide a loving home for their surviving children.

After the war during the Great Awakening, William Huntington Jr. found himself drawn to matters of faith and spirituality. He joined the Protestant Religious movement, seeking a deeper connection with God. Feeling called to live a purer life, he proudly gave up alcohol, tobacco, and hot drinks, believing it was a divine command.

Despite his initial enthusiasm, William grew disillusioned with the Protestant Church. He felt that something was missing and yearned for a return to the original Church that Christ had established. His study of the Bible led him to believe that a restoration of Christ's Church was not only necessary but imminent.

This belief gave William a renewed sense of purpose. He was determined to find and follow the true teachings of Christ, a quest that would soon lead him to profound and life-changing discoveries.

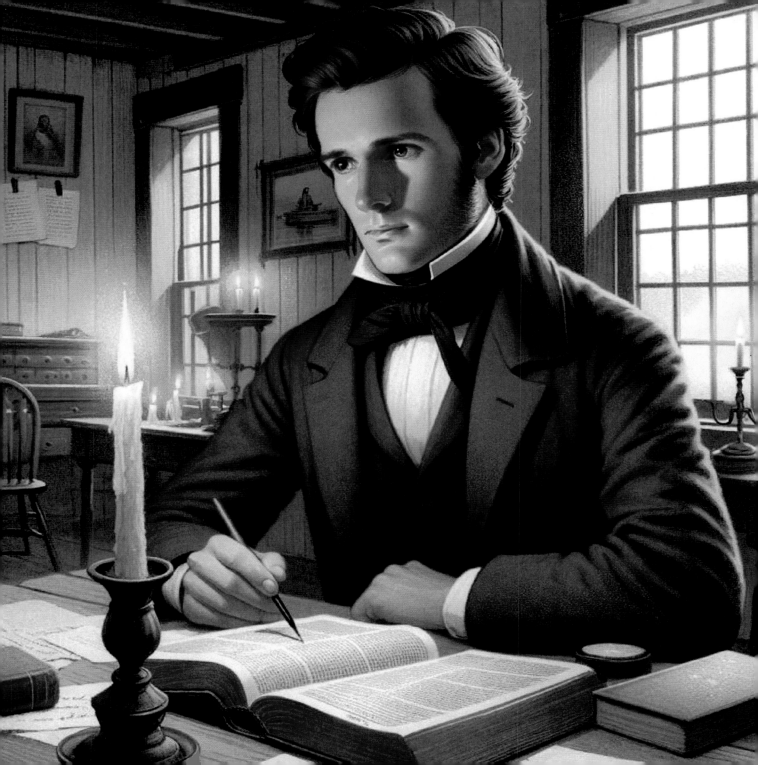

One evening, as the Huntington family gathered around the stove, singing hymns together, a stranger knocked on their door. Despite his haggard appearance and old clothing, they welcomed him in and offered him food. The stranger's presence felt oddly comforting and familiar.

As they conversed, the stranger began to explain the hymn they had been singing (Know This That Every Soul is Free) with remarkable insight. He then opened the scriptures and taught them profound truths they had never understood before. His words resonated deeply with William and his family, filling them with awe and wonder.

This experience reminded William of the feelings described in the New Testament by the disciples on the Road to Damascus. These were the truths that he had been seeking!

The stranger stayed the night and left quietly the next morning. Moments after he left, William sent his son after the stranger to invite him to stop by if he passed through the area again. When his son opened the door however, the stranger was gone and there were no footprints in the freshly fallen snow.

They often wondered about the stranger, and what had happened in their home on that special night. Despite the stranger's disappearance, the feelings and teachings that he left behind remained.

Years later William recounted the experience in the presence of Joseph Smith. Joseph surmised that the mysterious visitor was one of the Three Nephites, sent to prepare the Huntington family to receive the restored gospel. The Huntingtons never forgot their mysterious visitor.

Months after the visit from the mysterious stranger, the Huntington family welcomed another important guest into their home. Hyrum Smith, with his warm demeanor, brought a message that deeply resonated with them. He presented them with the Book of Mormon in 1833, a book that promised to answer the questions that had been troubling William for so long.

William and his family eagerly read the Book of Mormon and felt its truth. Inspired by the message, William spent all his free time sharing his newfound beliefs with friends and neighbors. The message of the restored gospel spread quickly, and soon William, Zina, and most of their children were baptized into the Church.

After three more years in New York, the family decided to join the Saints in Kirtland, Ohio. They sold everything they owned and traveled by steamboat, full of hope and excitement for the future.

The journey to Kirtland brought new challenges for the Huntington family. When the Kirtland Safety Society bank failed, William lost his land and found himself facing poverty once again. Despite this devastating setback, William and Zina remained steadfast in their faith.

Their neighbors, understanding their plight, loaned them oxen to pull their remaining supplies across the country to Missouri. It was a long and arduous journey, stretching over a thousand miles. William shipped some of their belongings ahead, but tragically, these never arrived, adding to their hardships.

Through it all, the Huntington family's determination never wavered. William would often say, referring to the Lord, "Swallow whatever the doctor gives you, for if he does not know what will cure you, nobody does."

Arriving in Missouri, William Huntington set his sights on settling his family in Adam-Ondi-Ahman, a place of great significance to the Saints. He left his family temporarily in Far West while he worked tirelessly to build their new home. The region, however, was fraught with danger as hostile mobs sought to drive the Saints away.

Every night, William slept with his rifle close by, ever vigilant and ready to defend his land and family. The constant threat of violence loomed over them, yet William's courage and dedication never faltered. He was determined to create a safe haven for his loved ones, no matter the cost.

The struggle to establish their home in Adam-Ondi-Ahman was a testament to the Huntington family's resilience and faith. Despite the dangers, they pressed on, driven by their belief in their purpose and mission.

William eventually succeeded in moving his family into the small, burgeoning community of Adam-Ondi-Ahman. For a time, it seemed like their struggles were paying off, and they were building a new life. However, this sense of security was short-lived. The Missouri state militia soon surrounded the town, demanding the surrender of all weapons and giving an ultimatum: the Saints must leave the state before spring.

The community was thrown into chaos. William was among those tasked with selling the land and belongings of the Saints. The hostile mobs knew they had the upper hand, often offering pitiful amounts for valuable properties. Despite his best efforts, William struggled to recover any significant funds, and the situation grew increasingly dire.

The forced evacuation was a heartbreaking ordeal for the Huntington family and their fellow Saints. They faced an uncertain future, driven from their homes once again by persecution and hatred.

In the spring, the Huntington family fled Missouri, seeking refuge in Quincy, Illinois. They arrived with little more than the clothes on their backs, living in absolute poverty. The harsh conditions took their toll, and one by one, family members fell ill.

The greatest blow came when Zina, William's beloved wife, succumbed to illness. Only one of their sons was well enough to attend her burial, a heartbreaking testament to the family's dire circumstances. William, devastated by grief and weakened by illness, struggled to carry on.

Joseph Smith and his family took William in, offering him shelter and care until he regained his strength. Their kindness and support were a beacon of hope during one of the darkest times in William's life.

Reflecting on his hardships, William recorded in his journal the profound impact of his trials: "...I had passed from a state of affluence worth thousands, down to the lowest state of poverty...My companion [was] gone, who had passed with me through all our trials and scenes of afflictions by water, by land, in war in Missouri, in moving to this place, in her sickness, to her death, and never murmured, nor complained. We felt to bear all our afflictions for Christ's sake, looking forward for the recompense of reward as did Paul through the goodness of God."

These words captured the depth of his sorrow and the strength of his faith. William found solace in the scriptures, drawing inspiration from the righteous men who had gone before him. Their examples provided him with the courage to endure and the hope for a brighter future.

In his darkest moments, William's unwavering belief in God's goodness and the promise of eternal rewards sustained him. His faith became a source of strength, guiding him through the toughest trials of his life.

After recovering from his illness, William wasted no time in getting back to work. He took up the trade of a stone mason, finding both purpose and livelihood in the skillful craft. In 1840, William's life took another significant turn when he married Lydia Partridge, the widow of Edward Partridge, the first bishop of the Church. Their union brought new companionship and mutual support.

In 1841, Joseph Smith introduced the doctrine of Baptism for the Dead, a teaching that resonated deeply with William. He embraced the practice with great joy, seeing it as a profound way to honor his ancestors. William was baptized on behalf of many deceased relatives, including his brother, grandfathers, and Samuel Huntington, a signer of the Declaration of Independence.

This new understanding and practice of faith brought William immense satisfaction. He felt a strong connection to his heritage and a renewed sense of spiritual fulfillment, knowing he was helping to bring his family closer to God.

William's sense of duty extended beyond his family and faith to his community. He served in the Nauvoo Legion, a local militia organized to protect the Saints from external threats. His role in the militia showcased his unwavering commitment to defending his community.

In addition to his military service, William contributed his skills as a stonemason to the construction of the Nauvoo Temple. He had the honor of laying the first cornerstone and later cutting the final stones used for the chimney. His craftsmanship showed his dedication and faith.

Despite the adversities he had faced, including losing everything twice, William's perseverance led to renewed prosperity. His hard work and faithfulness were rewarded, allowing him to rebuild and thrive once again.

The peace and prosperity in Nauvoo were short-lived as mobs once again began to threaten the Saints. The situation reached a tragic climax in 1844 with the murder of Joseph Smith. William, deeply saddened by the loss of their prophet and leader, was among the men chosen to help with Joseph's burial. The community was engulfed in grief and confusion.

Amidst this turmoil, discussions of moving westward to seek a place of peace and safety grew more urgent. The mobs' violence escalated, with homes and fields being set ablaze in the surrounding settlements. The need to leave Nauvoo became increasingly clear.

William was entrusted with the significant responsibility of leading a company of Saints out of Nauvoo. He began building wagons, preparing for their arduous journey westward. His leadership and dedication were crucial in these challenging times, as he helped his fellow Saints ready themselves for yet another exodus.

Even amidst the growing threats, the Saints completed the construction of the Nauvoo Temple. This sacred building became a beacon of hope and spiritual strength for the community. William was deeply honored to be among those administering the ordinances of the Endowment within its walls.

Administering these sacred ordinances brought William immense pride and fulfillment. He saw it as a way to empower his brethren and sisters with the spiritual strength they needed for the trials ahead. The Temple provided a place of refuge and divine connection, reinforcing their faith and unity.

The completion of the Temple and the ordinances performed within its walls were a symbol of the Saints' sacrifice and perseverance, even as they prepared to leave their beloved city.

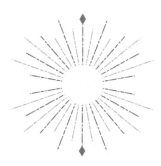

In early spring of 1846, William took on the critical task of leading his company of wagons out of Nauvoo. They crossed the Mississippi River, embarking on a grueling journey through snow and the wet, muddy conditions of the season. The journey was long and arduous, stretching over two months.

The travelers faced numerous challenges, including harsh weather and scarce resources. They camped in tents each night, often bartering for food and supplies with the communities they encountered along the way. William's leadership and resourcefulness were crucial in ensuring the group's survival and progress.

Finally, the weary travelers arrived at the settlement of Mount Pisgah. This temporary refuge provided them with a much-needed respite, allowing them to regroup and prepare for the next stage of their journey westward.

Upon arriving at Mount Pisgah, William's leadership and dedication were quickly recognized, and he was asked to serve as the Stake President. However, the trials and hardships of the journey had taken a severe toll on his health.

Tragically, William fell ill shortly after arriving at Mount Pisgah. Despite the best efforts of his family and fellow Saints, he passed away, leaving a profound void in the community. His passing was deeply mourned by all who knew him, as his commitment and faith had been a source of strength and inspiration.

William Huntington Jr.'s legacy lived on through the example he set and the lives he touched. His journey of faith, resilience, and unwavering dedication to his beliefs remained an enduring testament to his character and spirit.

William Huntington Jr.

A LIFE OF DEVOTION

MARCH 28,1784 -AUGUST 19, 1846

My Relationship:

FamilySearch.org ID: KWV9-4W1

Book Created for William's Great-Great-Great-Great Grandson, Gregg Huntington

Order More Copies at familyhistorystorybooks.com

Family History StoryBooks

Story by Jake Harmer
Illustrations by Jake Harmer
Photos obtained with permission by the family of the subject
1st edition 2024

Did You Like this Book?
Let us tell YOUR story!
Come visit us at familyhistorystorybooks.com and we can turn your own treasured stories into a children's book

SCAN ME

William Huntington Jr.

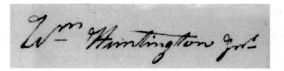

William's Signature

William Huntington Jr. Memorial Monument

Original Nauvoo Temple Star, which William may have carved

Letter written from William to Brigham Young from Mt. Pisgah

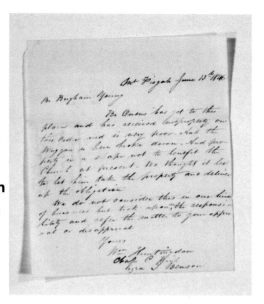

Wooden Chair built by William in the Nauvoo Era

Trowel used by William in construction of Nauvoo Temple

Made in the USA
Las Vegas, NV
10 October 2024

96633813R00024